Family, friendship and memories

Amisah Zenabu Bakuri

BookLeaf Publishing

India | USA | UK

Presentation by *BookLeaf Publishing*

Web: www.bookleafpub.com

E-mail: info@bookleafpub.com

ISBN: 9789357448185

First edition 2022

DEDICATION

To my Mother, Maria Amankwaa Mumuni, who gave me all I needed and much more,

To my husband, life partner and collaborator Daniel Antwi-Berko, you define love.

To our beloved children, Daniel, Dora Maria and Dromo, who have taught me what matters most in life.

ACKNOWLEDGEMENT

Thank you to all my friends and family,
for time spent together
for conversations
for love
for support
for encouragement

PREFACE

This book is a collection of poetry, I wrote while waiting to defend my PhD thesis. It is a reflection of my relationship with my family and friends. It also features my thoughts on conversations with friends and family about what was happening in their life.

My intention is to write a book that shows the beauty of simplicity in the things we say and do but also the joy, the pain, indecision, or the contentions therein.

I hope you have fun reading this book as much as I had fun writing the poems.

1. Birthday

Blow out the candles,
Cut the cake
See the mess of cream
Taste and eat your cake.
What's the taste like?
Is it sweet?
Is it nice?
Is it strange?
Or it's familiar?

Make a wish
Will it be a new one?
Or it's the old one?
Is it fashioned from all the ones you made years
ago?
Or it's just a new level of the old ones?
May it come to pass.

Did you make a wish list?
Like the one you made when you were three
years
The picture books
The colour pencils
The unicorn
The duplos

Or it's different, and you don't even remember
because you had a list of so many, like when you
turned four.
The paw patrols
Spiderman
Transformers
Bumblebee
Lego

Do you remember the pair of white sneakers you
wanted or the blue bike or the colourful skates?
Or the max Verstappen race car you saw on Tv
while watching your favourite sports program
with Daddy when you were five.
It is OK to tear all the wrapping paper and find
your new possessions
Are you happy?
Are you surprised?
Are you overwhelmed?
See all the colourful wrappers on the floor.
The different shades of blue, red and yellow
ribbons and wrappers
We wish for more birthdays
full of dreams come true and
fulfilment of your wishes
Tasting new cakes
Making lovely wishes

Unwrapping new presents and
Blowing the candles out

2. Taste heavenly

I like my sandwich and chocolate drink for my breakfast
But I love it when we eat it together
I sometimes forget to eat
Because you are not there
Don't get me wrong
I am not fasting
It just doesn't taste like when I eat it with you

And lunch
Yes, I prefer to have coffee sitting by my laptop, working.
Or having just a piece of fruit.
It can be a piece of mango, banana, some grapes, orange or an apple.
Or a candy or chocolate
I may quickly grab a sandwich or a biscuit
I know with you, it will be a bit more than just this. It may be a combination of these or fruit salad.
A little sandwich
And some candy
Yes, I am waiting for you to enjoy that lunch
I know I can eat my lunch alone, but I enjoy it with you.

It's dinner time
Food is ready
It's on the table
Well served
Well garnished
Looks yummy
I will wait for you
I am waiting because, with you, my food tastes
heavenly.

3.   Things I don't take for granted

When I say I love you
I mean it
It's not a phrase I throw around anyhow
I sincerely mean it

When I say thank you
I am grateful
I appreciate little things
And I am grateful for the big things
All you do for me it's appreciated

When I say God bless you
I say it with a prayer for you
You deserve blessings
Divine blessings

When I say I miss you
I say it from deep down my heart
Because I truly do
I miss you

I do not say these words and phrases just like
that
I mean them
And you only hear it when you deserve it

4. He popped the question

It was a question I had been waiting for. I wanted to see it on his lips. Perhaps he could put it in a letter. Maybe he should text me. I would instead love to hear him say it to me during one of our lunches. Will he say it during our walks? Was he going to ask during our study time? I saw him come to me all the time with beautiful stories and several questions. But I looked forward to one important one. I was sending all the clues, all the inactions and did not verbalise it. Should he ask me? Should he? Isn't it the right time? Does he want us to remain friends forever? But when he finally did? I did not want to say yes. I wanted him to wait a bit. Was he finally sure? Was he asking because he saw my impatience? Did he feel so, or was he just pressured? Anyways, I am happy you asked the question "I love you, Do you love me?"

5. Counting to ten is simple

We start counting
0,1,2
We enjoy counting
0,1,2,3...then
We got distracted
See, he has my painting
Give it to me
It's mine
He runs away with the painting
She starts crying
She gets all the attention
She remembers we were counting
She starts again
0,1,2, 3, 4

He joins in
5,6,7
No no no
Don't count with me
I don't want you counting with me
It's my 1,2, 3

It's not yours
We are family
We do things together
Not this my 1,2,3
Both laughing

Let us do it together
Maybe we can count it together
It's nice like that
1,2,3...
You made a mistake
It should start from 0
But you can also start from 1
They agree to start from 1
Because zero is not a number
But zero is a number
Indeed it depends on how you see it
Simple things can be complicated
And what counts may not count
What may not count may count

6. Dreams

How is the feeling like?
To lie in bed or stretching on the couch;
With ideas haunting you
With dreams
With imaginations
Staring at you,
Of all your past mistakes.
Of all the things you could have done right
Of the plans unaccomplished

Knowing you may not be able to set them right
You just keep dreaming
But you got to be hopeful!
Dreams do come true
Keep the hope alive

7. Mommy

Mommy is loving
Mommy has dreams
Mommy loves helping people
and live her many lives so she can help others
From counselling to nursing to teaching to
cooking to being an entrepreneur
She wears many hats and wears them well
Whichever hat she wears, she does her best

Mommy is a dreamer
A big dreamer
She dreams big
Hopes big
Have big fascination
She just doesn't dream
She works towards it
She prays about it
Seeks counsels
Read books
Talk to others

Mommy knows how to sacrifice to get her
dreams to come true
Be it sleepless nights
Selling off her things

Fasting and praying
Travellling
Learning new things
Advancing her knowledge

Mommy is a go-getter
She's so hopeful
She's a big dreamer
She's a firm believer
She's phenomenal

8. More than that!

You are yet to uncover her,
Her words
Her mannerisms
Her make-up
Her dressing
Her coloured fingernails
Her red lipstick
Her Rainbow eyeshadows
Her confidence

Forget her past
The memories,
or the pictures others took;
The stories others said—
Beneath this is more

9. Being genuinely loved

I genuinely hope you feel loved,
And get the affection you need,
And get the attention you want
And get the love you deserve

Not just from the nannies
Not just from mummy and daddy's friends
Not just from grandma and grandpa
But from your own parents.
It's not just about the money
It's not just about the "help."
It's not just about any care.

It's about the emotions
It's about affections
It's about friendships
It's about care
It's about genuine love

10. All of me

Don't love me for only what your eyes would
see.
Don't love me for only what you will hear about
me
Don't love me for only what others say about me
Don't love me for only what I do for you
Don't love me for only what I have
Don't love me for what I can do

If you do,
You will only love me for my words
You will only love me by what I have
You will only love me for what you have heard
You will only love me for what I can do

I want you to love me for who I am, who I can
be and what I can do or not do.
Love me for all of me
Love me for my words
Love me for what you know
Love my body, my words, my actions, my
inactions, my heart, my thoughts and my flaws.
Love all of me.

11. I am

I am attractive.
I am beautiful
I am wise
I am talented
I am strong
I am bold
I am confident
I am lucky.
I am healthy
I am blessed
I am a great learner.
I am an overcomer.
I am a conqueror
I am a great wife
I am a good mother
I am a supportive friend

Do not joke with your "I am's."
What follows those two simple words
Should be what you really are
It should not be about just a moment or an
incident
Don't make a mistake out of your mouth tumbles
Invite positive I am
You are fearfully and wonderfully made.

12. Hello sleep

Hello sleep
When are you coming?
I have been waiting
Waiting in bed
Waiting now on my couch

Why are you delaying
Is it because of the music I am listening to?
Is it because of the book I am reading?
Or the song that lives rent-free in my head?
Is it because I am overindulging?
Or is it because I have so much on my mind?

My mind is preoccupied.
Preoccupied with my plans
Preoccupied with unaccomplished dreams
Preoccupied with the pain of being stuck
I have cried
I have tried
I cuddled

Hello sleep
Are you finally here?
Here to give me a short nap

Here to give my body a little rest
Here to help me stop wandering in my mind
Please take me away momentarily from my
worries

13. Time

We ran
We remove the high heels
No time to wear the sneakers
We ran barefoot
We remove our jackets
It's getting hectic

We cry out to God
Our digital maps are giving all of us different
directions
What do we do?
How do we start a journey of 15 mins an hour
earlier and end up late?
Time!, time is not on our side.

Why its time running away from us
Time run towards us
We shout out
We cry even louder

Will this bike take us to the location?
See all those bikes parked in the streets of
Amsterdam
But it's locked.

It is not our bike

Look at the water
Can we swim there
None of us can swim
What!!!!
We don't want to be wet.
We keep running

How I wish I could just pull one of the scooter
riders to give us a ride
I start imagining the scenes on TV?
Those where people could just push riders off
And drive away in the heat of the moment.
That is not possible.
We keep moving.

I momentarily wish we could fly?
Glide to the place
Fly like the birds in the sky
Perhaps fly like angels
We don't have wings
God, please send us wings

I come back to myself.
Wishes are not horses.
I was a beggar to ride now
Perhaps we needed a horse
To ride fast to the venue

We are getting frustrated.
Becoming emotional
Becoming impatient
Running and hoping to bike, swim or fly or even
vanish there
We keep running, trying to calm ourselves

The bride is tired
How we wish we could carry her
She keeps running
Running amidst speeches from bridesmaids
Maid of honour tries to calm her

We can't stop
It is 5 minutes away
What a big miss, if we don't keep running
We feel tired
It is 4 minutes away
With each footstep into the floor
We imagine different possibilities
It is 2 minutes away
I think of the kisses, the love notes, the
speeches, the toast she might miss

We run even faster,
Knowing every second counts
Time! Time! Time!

Run towards us
Would you mind running towards us?

We made it
On time
Everyone calming the bride
It started slowly and ended beautifully
We begin to make jokes about it all

It was emotionally draining
But that time passed, and we laughed
With kisses
With hugs
Time was now on our side
Let's party!

14. Play

If I could play all-day
Put the play into words
Or put my play in writing
Perhaps sing it
Feel these games
Would it warm my heart?
Or make me reel?

There are so many games.
I just want to play
Constantly playing
So many that I am still discovering
The old ones I don't want to throw away
Or those I would savour
I am indecisive -
Which one is best?

It's challenging to decide.
I like to play
All the time
But with many games
I am left with so many options
Old games bring memories
Some bring a flood of raw emotions
New games bring me excitement

I have a pile of games
I just want to play
But I struggle to decide -
which one to play

15. Pain

This writing is painful
A painful process I want to complete
This pain makes me cry
This pain makes me feel sad
It hurts
It is unbearable
It sometimes feels lonely

And the words in my head- are not those I write
The words in my heart - I cannot write
What I am thinking- May not be suitable to write
What I write- Its misread
What I write- its misunderstood
What I write- it's not enough
What I write- cannot let me pass the process
What I write- does not count
I rewrite

They say it's few steps forward
They say after I go forward
I should go few steps backwards
But to go through the process, I need to move
forward
It looks like I am stuck
No one can unstuck me

I am unable to help myself
I cry

I try
I stop
I continue
I share my writing
I share my insecurities
I am sharing my vulnerabilities
Do I love to share these?
They say that it is the process
I need the result

I strive to go through this painful process
This pain is a necessary part of this process
Do I quit because of the pain?
Or continue through the pain?
A rewarding pain is still pain.
I look at those who have gone through the pain
They shine on
I want to shine, but I wish I would not go
through such pain
I will try

16. Happiness

No one MUST make me happy
I MUST make myself happy
But I am happy you make me happy
I am happy you try all within your means for me
I am happy you are by my side
I am happy you say you love me always
I am happy you show me you love me always
I am happy you buy me the flowers
I am happy you get me the gifts
I am happy you are always there for me
I am happy you put up with my moods
I am happy you sacrifice a lot for me
But are you happy?

17. Our flower is a tree now

Daddy, you left
No goodbye
No goodbye hugs and kisses
You just left
I needed you
I miss you
I stared at the flower you had given me
It withered slowly
It withered one by one
I understood you wanted me to grow it
I started watering it
Day by day, I took care of it
Because it was from you
It's a tree now!

18. Broken and fixed

I was broken
Thank God that I am fixed
Handle me with lots of care
If I brake again
There might be missing pieces
Then I may not be fixable

19. Finding faults?

She's home
Trying to find a problem
There is no problem
But she's searching
Big sis says mum, you won't find any problem
Kid bro laughs, she's loading them, it's 20%...
We tell her to stop downloading problems
There aren't any in this house
We kept it as you left it
Mum disconnects her search
We all sigh
What a relief!

20. We choose each
other

You could be a professor somewhere
A doctor elsewhere
A pastor
A lecturer
Manager
Author
Scientists
Writer
Counsellor
Entrepreneur
Motivational speaker
You could be anything anywhere

But you decide to be with me,
Go where I go
You decide to be mine forever
Let's achieve our dreams together
Too many sacrifices for me

You tell me I am enough
I see that indeed you don't regret
You don't look back

Neither do you look sideways
You only look forward with me

I appreciate it
I love you
You can be anything in the world
I will be right beside you.

21. Giving up

I can't give up
Because you look up to me

I can't give up
Because you are counting on me

I can't give up
Because I count on you counting on me

I can't give up
Because when you count on me

Like 1,2,3…
I should be there

www.ingramcontent.com/pod-product-compliance
Lightning Source LLC
Chambersburg PA
CBHW070613160726
48003CB00005B/2246